I0500154

# THE 6 FINANCIAL
# LAWS OF SUCCESS

## THE SECRETS MILLIONAIRES KNOW
## THAT POOR PEOPLE DON'T

Christopher Mitchell

www.ChangeYourLifeOvernight.com

*THE 6 FINANCIAL LAWS OF SUCCESS:*
*THE SECRETS MILLIONAIRES KNOW THAT*
*POOR PEOPLE DON'T*

Copyright © 2017 Christopher Mitchell

ISBN-13: 978-1548190552

ISBN-10: 1548190551

Unless otherwise noted, all scriptures quoted are from the New International Version (NIV) of The Holy Bible. Copyright 1973, 1978, 1984, 2011 by Biblica, Inc. Used by permission. All rights reserved worldwide.

**All rights reserved**. Under International Copyright Law no part of this publication may be reproduced, stored in a retrieval system or transmitted in any form- digital, electronic, mechanical, photocopy, recording or any other form without the prior written permission of the author or publisher.

**Printed In The United States Of America**.

# TABLE OF CONTENTS:

Christopher hopes this book will educate and inspire you to change your life financially forever. By following the laws explained throughout this book, you will absolutely create more money in your life. Money is good because you can't live without it. The more money you have access to means the more people you can be a blessing to. If you want to speak to Christopher, or perhaps join his team and have him become your personal mentor, feel free to contact him at his website listed here. God bless you!

www.ChangeYourLifeOvernight.com

# Chapter One:

## *Tithing*

The Law Of Tithing states that you should give 10% of your gross income to your home church. It's really quite simple. If you earn $100,000 per year that means you would tithe $10,000 or $833 per month. However, only about 3% of the world's population tithe and only 2% of the world's population are wealthy. So, you put two and two together. According to www.StateOfThePlate.info, only ten million people out of the three hundred fifteen million who live in The United States are tithers. If you do the math that equals about 3%. Numbers never lie. Every wealthy person I've ever met tithes their income. Tithers are generous people and generous people prosper. It even says this verbatim in the Holy Bible:

*A generous person will prosper; whoever refreshes others will be refreshed.* **Proverbs 11:25**

Tithers are wealthy people and the numbers prove it. Tithing isn't just for Christians by the way. Tithing is a universal principle. Tithing is a law that works for everyone no matter what their religious beliefs are. People who give away their money have money come back to them in multiplied amounts, usually from unknown sources. However, people who don't give away their money are stingy and stingy people are poor. This is confirmed in the Holy Bible:

*The stingy are eager to get rich and are unaware that poverty awaits them.* **Proverbs 28:22**

Poor people need to understand in order to become wealthy they must change their mindset and habits about money. What you give away will always come back to you. This is another law that I'll talk about later in this book. However, poor people always complain about the rich, but they could just as easily become rich themselves if they would start being generous with their money instead of hoarding it. Tithing is giving and poor people must start giving money if they ever want to become wealthy.

Not only do poor people not give to others, but they don't even give to God. Everywhere a person goes in this world costs money. When you go to the grocery store you can't walk out without first leaving some money behind. When you go to a restaurant you can't walk out without first leaving some money behind. When you go to the movie theaters you can't walk out without first leaving some money behind. When you go to a sporting event you can't walk out without first leaving some money behind. Shoot, most of these places won't even allow you to walk in without first giving them some of your money. However, poor people have no problem going to church, listen to the Senior Pastor preach an Academy Award winning sermon, and then walk out without leaving any money behind. That is stinginess! Let me remind you again what happens to people who are stingy:

*The stingy are eager to get rich and are unaware that poverty awaits them.* **Proverbs 28:22**

If you want to become wealthy do what wealthy people do. Wealthy people tithe. Poor people say that rich people tithe because they're better off, but rich people say they're better off because they tithe.

Researchers compared the finances of tithers to non-tithers using nine financial health indicators and found that tithers were better off in every single category. Among the group of tithers, 80% don't have any credit card debt, 74% don't owe anything on their cars, 48% don't owe anything on their homes, and 28% of them are completely debt free. Again, numbers don't lie. You decide for yourself if it makes sense to start tithing. To me, the results are quite obvious.

I didn't intend on writing this book from a religious perspective, but I do need to reference the Holy Bible from time to time because it's the best book on wealth creation ever written. It's the number one best-selling book of all time and every millionaire and billionaire I've ever met refer to it on a regular basis. So, I think it's very important to mention what it says.

*Ever since the time of your ancestors you have turned away from my decrees and have not kept them. Return to me, and I will return to you, says the Lord Almighty. But you ask, how are we to return? Will a mere mortal rob God? Yet you rob me. But you ask, how are we robbing you? In tithes and offerings. You are under a curse, your whole nation because you are robbing me. Bring the whole tithe into the storehouse, that there may be food in my house. Test me in this, says the Lord Almighty, and see if I will not throw open the floodgates of heaven and pour out so much blessing that there will not be room enough to store it.* **Malachi 3:7-10**

Let me ask you a question based on the set of scriptures above. Are you a tither or non-tither? If you're a non-tither, are you cursed financially? Do you live paycheck to paycheck?

If you don't give tithes, but you live paycheck to paycheck, you might want to rethink this concept called tithing. All the millionaires and billionaires in the world who tithe can't be wrong. Tithing is a secret that rich people know that poor people don't. Well, poor people do know about it, they just choose not to acknowledge it. By not tithing you're choosing to stay poor.

I want to remind you everywhere a person goes they must leave some of their money behind. The tithe is the first thing a person should release whenever they have money come to them. Instead of thinking that you can't afford to tithe you need to change your mindset and start thinking that you can't afford NOT to tithe. When fear starts creeping into your mind remember the difference between the tithers and non-tithers.

Tithing is not a financial issue. It's a trust issue. A tither says: God, I trust you to do what you said you would do, so here's a token of my faith. God asks you to trust him with some of your money because he knows that it's the most valuable thing to you. He doesn't want money to be your God because he knows that the love of money is the root of all kinds of evil. Money is a terrible God, but an awesome servant. When you refuse to tithe you're admitting that money is your God. It has a stronghold on you and you'll never become rich. Again, what does the Holy Bible say:

*No one can serve two masters. Either you will hate the one and love the other, or you will be devoted to the one and despise the other. You cannot serve both God and money.*
**Matthew 6:24**

*One person gives freely, yet gains even more, another withholds unduly, but comes to poverty.* **Proverbs 11:24**

*Whoever can be trusted with very little can also be trusted with much, and whoever is dishonest with very little will also be dishonest with much.* **Luke 16:10**

Poor people say they love and trust God, but then refuse to give him just 10% of their income. God knows that talk is cheap. He also knows that your actions speak louder than words. Don't say you love and trust God with your words, but then rob him by not paying your tithes with your actions. You can't lie to God. He knows your heart. He wants to bless you, but he can't if you're going to choose money above him. Become a tither and the floodgates of heaven will open up for you in your finances.

# Chapter Two:

## *Attraction*

The Law Of Attraction states that whatever you focus on you're going to attract into your life because your thoughts are things. Attraction could also be called visualization. What are you visualizing on a regular basis? Do you visualize getting bills in the mail every day or do you visualize getting paychecks in the mail every day? Based on what you're getting in the mail every day will tell you what you constantly focus on.

Do you ever focus on getting caught in a traffic jam on the freeway? If so, what happens? You get caught in a traffic jam don't you? Do you ever focus on arriving late to work in the morning? If so, what happens? You arrive late to work don't you?

I can always look back to my past and figure out what I was focusing on during that time period based on what I was attracting into my life. I was playing in one of my baseball games when I was sixteen years old and I remember seeing a beautiful girl with blonde hair watching the game from the bleachers. I stared at her when I walked up to the plate when it was my turn to bat. I stared at her when I was in the field playing shortstop. I stared at her when I ran off the field to the dugout when the innings were over. I had never seen her before, but I couldn't get her out of my mind. I didn't know her name. I didn't know who she was. I didn't even know who she was cheering for. All I knew is that I wanted to meet her, talk to her, and go out on a date with her. By the time the game was over and I packed up my equipment, she was gone. She was nowhere to be found. I thought about her later that night. I thought about her while I was in school. I thought about her when I was at baseball practice. I thought about her all the time.

About a month later, I received a random phone call. When I answered the phone the voice of an unknown female asked for me by name. I asked her who she was. She said, I'm the blonde girl that was sitting in the bleachers watching your baseball game about a month ago. What? I yelled in excitement! Are you kidding me? How in the world did you get my phone number? How did you find out who I was? What are you calling me for? She said, I thought you were cute. I wanted to talk to you after your game, but I had to leave. So, I started asking around. Sure enough, I tracked you down.

That's amazing I said! I'm so glad you did. I haven't stopped thinking about you since that day. We started dating at that very moment. That story clearly shows you how powerful our thoughts are. I focused on her for an entire month. She didn't even go to my school, but my laser beam, focused thoughts attracted her into my life. What I focused on, which is also known as The Law Of Attraction, works every single time!

As a little boy growing up I loved the Rocky movies played by Sylvester Stallone. I must have watched those movies at least one hundred times. I knew every single word in every movie. I visualized myself being Rocky in the movies. I would punch the same way that he punched. I would talk the same way that he talked. I would even mimic every move that he made. I focused on playing the role of Rocky by Sylvester Stallone so often that he started to dominate my thoughts. I wanted to meet him so badly. I wanted to tell him how much I loved watching his movies.

Well, years later when I was in my twenties I worked as a vendor at a supplement booth in Columbus, Ohio at the annual Arnold Schwarzenegger Bodybuilding Expo. While walking through thousands of people to get to my booth I suddenly came across a huge mob of people blocking all the walk ways. I was surrounded by people and there was nowhere to go. I asked some people crammed up next to me what was going on? They said, Sylvester Stallone is about fifty yards ahead.

OMG! I couldn't believe it. The man I idolized growing up as a little boy was now fifty yards in front me? Are you serious? I knew this was my moment. I knew this was my chance, but how would I ever meet him when he's surrounded by security guards and thousands of fans? I didn't know the answer, but I did know without a doubt in my mind I was going to meet him that day. I remembered this amazing story in The Holy Bible:

In Luke 8:43-48, the Holy Bible talks about the woman who had the issue of blood. She wanted her healing. She visualized her healing. She knew that if she could just reach out and touch Jesus she would be healed. However, she had a problem. Jesus was in the middle of thousands of people. That didn't matter to her though. She was determined to make her way through all those people and nothing was going to stop her from getting her healing. Sure enough, she put The Law Of Attraction to work. She didn't focus on what she didn't want, which was having to get through thousands of people. She only focused on what she did want, which was touching Jesus so she could be healed. She received her healing as soon as she touched him. What she focused on, which is also known as The Law Of Attraction, works every single time!

My situation was similar. I focused on getting to Sylvester Stallone that day as much as that woman focused on getting to Jesus. I was determined. Nothing was going to stop me. Sure enough, I made my way through thousands of people that day and got to meet Sylvester Stallone and even had my picture taken with him. I received exactly what I focused on. What I focused on, which is also known as The Law Of Attraction, works every single time!

One of my all time favorite scriptures that I live by every single day is:

*Do not conform to the pattern of this world, but be transformed by the renewing of your mind.* **Romans 12:2**

This verse tells us not to think like the rest of the world thinks, but to renew our minds and start thinking the way that God thinks. The rest of the world would have given up in the previous situations. They would have focused on the obstacle, not on the prize. If you want to become a Millionaire you must renew your mind by changing the way you think. If you want to lose weight, gain energy, and increase strength, you have to feed your body with nutritious foods. In the same way, to change the way you think you have to start feeding your mind with nutritious thoughts. You do this by reading positive, self-help books.

Back in 2007, I was living in Chicago, Illinois. While I was driving to an event in Columbus, Ohio, my tires ran over some black ice. In a matter of seconds, my life changed for the worse. My passenger and I woke up to the sounds of sirens and the jaws of life cutting my car to pieces. My car was demolished. By the grace of God, we lived. It took a while to recover, but today we're both fine.

During my healing time, I started renewing my mind to the word of God. I started focusing on what I wanted and believed it was coming to me. I received a six-figure job offer as a personal trainer with a company in Orlando, Florida. However, I had a few problems. I didn't have a car, I didn't have any money, and I didn't have good credit. How was I going to be able to get a car so I could drive back and forth to my new job?

I knew that it looked impossible for me to get a new car in the natural, but I also knew that what I focus on I get. So, instead of focusing on not having any money or good credit, I only focused on getting a new car.

At this point in my life I didn't have the prosperous mindset that I have today. So, instead of focusing on a Lamborghini, I focused on a much less expensive car. I walked to the Honda dealership in downtown Chicago. I found a brand new, sparkling red, 2008 Honda Civic sitting on the showroom floor. That's the car I wanted. I accepted it by faith right then and there. A car salesman walked up to me and I told him this was the car I wanted. He told me to follow him back to his desk. He asked me if I had good credit for financing and I told him no I didn't. He then asked me, how do you think you're going to get a brand new car with bad credit? I told him I didn't know how, but I knew that my God would deliver it. He rolled his eyes at me.

He had me fill out a credit application hoping that I might get approved anyway. After he ran my credit he realized I was telling him the truth. He told me there was no way I was going to be able to get that car. I smiled and told him with God ALL things are possible! I then left the dealership. As I walked away I started visualizing myself sitting in the car, driving the car, and enjoying the car in the Florida sun. This intense focusing is a very real process. When you focus on something with great intensity it makes it feel like you already have the thing that you're focusing on. I can't explain the feeling in words, but I just knew without a shadow of doubt the car was mine.

I bought a plane ticket from Chicago to Orlando with every last penny that I had. I would arrive in Orlando on Friday and start working at my new job on Monday morning. In my spirit, I just knew, that I knew, that I knew, that somehow, someway, I was going to get that brand new Honda Civic. I just didn't know how. That's ok though. I knew The Law Of Attraction worked, so I just kept focusing on having the car in my possession. I would leave the rest up to God.

On Friday morning, just hours before I would fly to Orlando, I received the following email that said this:

Hi Christopher, you don't know me, but I met you a few years ago in Columbus, Ohio at the Arnold Schwarzenegger Bodybuilding Expo. I got a copy of the bodybuilding magazine that you were on the cover of that month and you autographed it for me. I only talked to you for a few minutes because other people were waiting in line to meet you. However, you were the nicest bodybuilder I had ever met. I just wanted to say it was a pleasure to meet you. If you ever need anything please feel free to contact me anytime. Sincerely, Bill.

That was the exact email that I received from Bill. The thing that jumped out of his email the most was: If you ever need anything please feel free to contact me anytime. I thought to myself, well, I need a car. Bill just told me that if I ever needed anything to contact him. So, I decided to email him back and fill him in.

I told him I was in a bad car crash. I told him I just got offered a six figure position as a personal trainer in Florida, but I didn't have a car to get back and forth once I got there. I asked him if he would pray for me that God would somehow bring me a car. That's all I said to him. Within one hour he emailed me back with the following message:

Christopher, I'm so sorry to hear about what happened to you. I know you don't know me, but I'm the CEO of a bank. I have perfect credit and plenty of money. You left such an impression on me when I met you that I would be happy to buy you a car. Please call me! Sincerely, Bill.

To make a long story short, he told me to go to the Honda dealership once I arrived in Orlando. When I picked out the car that I wanted call him and put him on the phone with the salesman. He said he would take care of the rest. I went to the Honda dealership as soon as I arrived in

Orlando. I found the same exact, brand new, sparkling red, 2008 Honda Civic sitting on the showroom floor that I saw on the showroom floor in Chicago. I called Bill, put him on the phone with the car salesman, and two hours later I drove off that car lot with a brand new car without paying a penny for it. It was an unbelievable experience! I drove into an empty parking lot and started to cry. I couldn't believe the way God had come through for me. He used a complete stranger to buy me a brand new car. I think I would have had better odds winning the lottery than to have that happen to me, but it did. God is truly amazing!

I had my part to play though and that's where most people miss it. I had to focus on what I wanted, confess it with my mouth, receive it by faith, then trust in God to bring it to me, which he did in the most unbelievable way a person ever could have imagined. What I focused on, which is also known as The Law Of Attraction, works every single time!

Here's a visualization method you can use to focus on what you want in life. Lay down on your back in a quiet place with no distractions. Imagine yourself laying on the shore of the ocean. Your feet are closest to the water. Inhale deep breaths. As you breathe in imagine the waves are coming in toward you. As you breathe out imagine the waves going back out to sea. With each breath you take calm those waves down until the water is completely still. Now you're breathing should be very relaxed. This is a deep meditative state that you're in. Now, begin to visualize the life you want. Mentally see yourself driving your dream car, living in your dream home, having the perfect physical body, traveling the world to all your favorite places, giving millions of dollars away to the needy, and even being healed from sickness and disease. Whatever it is that you desire, visualize it and make it real right now! The more you focus on the life you want, the faster it will manifest in the natural world.

## Chapter Three:

*Confession*

The Law Of Confession states that the words you speak will manifest in your life because your words are seeds. Every single word you speak is either bringing you closer to your goals and dreams or taking you further away from your goals and dreams. Most people use The Law Of Confession against themselves because they don't even realize that their words have power. It is so important to only speak words that describe the life you want, not the life you don't want. The written word of God, which is the Holy Bible, is filled with empowering scriptures that I encourage you to start confessing with your mouth on a daily basis. Believing and speaking the word of God is a very powerful law that can truly change your life.

God created the entire universe by the power of his words. He gave us this same power to use in our lives as well. Let me show you here.

*God **said**, let there be light and there was light.* **Genesis 1:3**

*God **said**, let there be a vault between the waters to separate water from water.* **Genesis 1:6**

*God **said**, let the water under the sky be gathered to one place and let dry ground appear.* **Genesis 1:9**

*God **said**, let the land produce vegetation; seed bearing plants and trees on the land that bear fruit with seed in it according to their various kinds.* **Genesis 1:11**

*God **said**, let there be lights in the vault of the sky to separate the day from the night, and let them serve as signs to mark sacred times, days and* *years, and let them be lights in the vault of the sky to give light on the earth.* **Genesis 1:14-15**

*God **said**, let the water teem with living creatures and let birds fly above the earth across the vault of the sky.* **Genesis 1:20**

*God **said**, let the land produce living creatures according to their kinds: the livestock, the creatures that move along the ground, and the wild animals each according to its kind.* **Genesis 1:24**

*God **said**, let us make mankind in our image, in our likeness, so that they may rule over the fish in the sea and the birds in the sky, over the livestock and all the wild animals, and over all the creatures that move along the ground.* **Genesis 1:26**

This is amazing! Not only did God create the entire universe simply by speaking it into existence, but he created you in his image and likeness. That means he gave you the same exact power and authority with the words that you speak. Your words have amazing power. Your words can literally change any circumstance in your life. That's why it's extremely important to only speak about things that you want. Don't ever speak about things that you don't want. The words that you speak **WILL** manifest in your life!

When we were growing up as children we always heard the saying: *sticks and stones will break my bones, but words will never hurt me*. As adults, we know the complete opposite is true. Sticks and stones have never broken any bones, but hurtful words have been known to cause people all kinds of problems. Some people have even committed murder and suicide because of the power of someone's words. Children who have parents that speak negatively to them all the time grow up with inferiority complexes. So, if you're a parent make sure you only speak positive and uplifting words to your children. Remind them with your words that they're blessed and they can achieve anything they set their mind to. The majority of people in the world are poor because of the powerful words they speak.

Do you ever notice that poor people always say things like:

-I can't afford that.

-Money is the root of all evil.

-Money doesn't grow on trees.

-I'd rather be happy than be rich.

Every time a person speaks negative words about money they're only cursing themselves financially. They're setting themselves up to be poor forever. If you say you can't afford something you're absolutely right. You'll never be able to afford it.

Instead of confessing how poor you are all the time start confessing how rich you are. Jesus came to give us life and give it to us in abundance. Abundance isn't living a life of poverty. Abundance is being rich. Abundance is having more than enough. Abundance is having so much that your cup runs over.

Start confessing what the Holy Bible says about your finances instead of what your bank statements say about your finances. Confessing God's word over your finances will change what your bank statements say. Stop trying to figure out how your circumstances are going to change and just start confessing what God's word says. You don't have to know how. All you need to know is that confessing God's word will change any situation in the natural world if you'll simply believe what you speak. That's how The Law Of Confession works. You have to believe and then speak the word of God! Let's see what the Holy Bible says about the power of our words:

*My word that goes out from my mouth will not return to me empty, but will accomplish what I desire and achieve the purpose for which I sent it.* **Isaiah 55:11**

*The tongue has the power of life and death, and those who love it will eat its fruit.* **Proverbs 18:21**

*By your words you will be acquitted, and by your words you will be condemned.* **Matthew 12:37**

*If I say to this mountain, go throw yourself into the sea, and do not doubt in my heart, but believe what I say will happen, it will be done for me.* **Mark 11:23**

*I give life to the dead and call into being things that were not.*
**Romans 4:17**

*Do not let any unwholesome talk come out of your mouth, but only what is helpful for building others up according to their needs, that it may benefit those who listen.*
**Ephesians 4:29**

I remember telling people when I was only seventeen years old that I was going to become a professional fitness model and appear on the covers of fitness magazines all over the world. Every single person I said that to laughed at me and told me I was crazy. However, I kept confessing over and over to myself that I would appear on the covers of fitness magazines. A year later, when I was eighteen years old, I appeared on my first magazine cover. I had spoken that into existence just like God spoke the entire universe into existence. Our words are powerful.

If you have a car loan, a mortgage loan, or credit card loans, that means you're in debt! Use The Law Of Confession to get yourself out of debt. Take your car loan, your mortgage loan, and your credit card loans and speak to them. Listen up car loan, I command that you be completely paid off in the name of Jesus! Listen up mortgage loan, I command that you be completely paid off in the name of Jesus! Listen up credit card loans, I command that you be completely paid off in the name of Jesus!

Use The Law Of Confession to bring in more money. Open up your empty purse or wallet and speak to it. Listen up purse, I command that you are now filled with hundred dollar bills. I command that you now overflow with money. I command that money comes to me from the north, south, east, and west.

Use The Law Of Confession to reprogram your poverty mindset into a prosperous mindset. Look yourself in the mirror every single day and repeat out loud: I am rich! I am prosperous! I am successful! I am a Multi-Millionaire! Money comes to me easily and abundantly every single day! My sales are increasing every single day! New opportunities come to me every single day! I am the lender and not the borrower. I am happy, healthy, and extremely wealthy! Everything I do prospers and succeeds. I love money and money loves me! Money comes to me easily!

Don't think you're too good to look at yourself in the mirror and talk to yourself like this. Look at the power of what your words can do. Your words can absolutely eliminate your debt and bring in huge sums of money supernaturally from places you can't even imagine. But, you have to BELIEVE what you speak! Jesus knew his words were powerful. He killed a fig tree with his words.

*The next day as they were leaving Bethany, Jesus was hungry. Seeing in the distance a fig tree in leaf, he went to find out if it had any fruit. When he reached it, he found nothing but leaves because it was not the season for figs. Then he said to the tree, may no one ever eat fruit from you again. And his disciples heard him say it.* **Mark 11:12-14**

Believe it, then speak it! Your words can change your entire life. You must start paying attention to every word that comes out of your mouth. There is nothing in the entire world that cannot be turned around by the power of your words. Most people don't understand the connection between the words they speak and the lives they live. Look at another amazing scripture that Jesus spoke:

*The Spirit gives life, the flesh counts for nothing. The words I have spoken to you, they are full of the Spirit and life.* **John 6:63**

# Chapter Four:

## *Association*

The Law Of Association states that whoever you associate with is who you will soon become. Who do you currently associate with?

-People who give or take?

-People who love or hate?

-People who are rich or poor?

-People who read or watch TV?

-People who are honest or liars?

-People who worship Jesus or Satan?

I highly encourage you to answer each one of those questions honestly. It will show you why your life is what it currently is. More importantly than that, it will show you who you need to eliminate from your life if you wish to take your life to another level.

It's impossible for you to be a giver if everyone you associate with is a taker. It's impossible for you to be a lover if everyone you associate with is a hater. It's impossible for you to be rich if everyone you associate with is poor. It's impossible for you to be a reader if everyone you associate with watches TV. It's impossible for you to be honest if everyone you associate with tells lies. It's impossible for you to be lean, healthy, and energetic if everyone you associate with is fat and unhealthy. It's impossible for you to worship Jesus if everyone you associate with worships Satan. This is true because The Law Of Association states that whoever you associate with is who you will soon become. We've heard from early childhood that: *birds of a feather flock together*. This is The Law Of Association!

People only associate with people they have things in common with. Do you ever see Bill Gates associating with homeless people on the street? No, of course not! But, why not? Because they don't have anything in common. What would they talk about? Homeless people are begging for spare change and Bill Gates makes $1.2 million dollars every single hour.

When you're driving out in the country and come across a chicken coop, do you ever see any eagles on the ground pecking with all the chickens? No, of course not! But, why not? Because they don't have anything in common. Chickens walk on the ground, but eagles soar in the sky. Do you want to be a chicken in life or an eagle? 98% of the world's population are chickens. They don't even try to soar. They're perfectly content pecking on the ground.

They're perfectly content working from dark thirty in the morning until dark thirty at night at their dead end jobs. They're perfectly content getting paid twenty dollars per hour. They're perfectly content getting a thirty-minute lunch break. They're perfectly content being away from their family members for eight to twelve hours every day. They're perfectly content watching TV for five hours every night when they get home from work. They're perfectly content with being fat and out of shape. They're perfectly content living in a piece of crap house. They're perfectly content driving a piece of junk car. They're perfectly content making a house payment for thirty years. They're perfectly content being poor. Chickens are always content living a pathetic existence. However, eagles are never content.

Eagles were created to soar high above the chickens. Eagles only associate with other eagles. Eagles are leaders. Eagles look at what everyone else in the world is doing and do the exact opposite. Eagles have strong vision. Eagles are over achievers always looking to accomplish more. Eagles are very rare. They make up less than 1% of the population in the world. Whether you're a chicken or an eagle is simply a choice. Why do so many people in the world choose to be chickens when they could just as easily choose to be eagles? The reason why is because they associate with other chickens every day. They've become who they associate with.

If you're a parent you know how important it is to keep your children away from the so-called "bad" kids. You know that if your children associate with the wrong people that could have a devastating effect on who they become in life. Influence is a very powerful thing in this world. If your children get influenced by the wrong people they could get hooked on alcohol, cigarettes, and illegal, recreational drugs.

The same is true for adults. If you associate with someone who is constantly sleeping around and cheating on their spouse, that's exactly what you're going to do. If you associate with people who drink beer at the bar every night, that's exactly what you're going to do. However, if you associate with people who are happy, healthy, and wealthy, then you too will become happy, healthy, and wealthy. That's how The Law Of Association works.

You must always remember that: *birds of a feather flock together*. You will always do, be, and have what your associations do, be, and have. The Law Of Association is a very powerful law. I have seen many people throughout my lifetime who have ruined their lives because of the people they associated with. I have seen people become smokers because they associated with people who smoke. I have seen people become alcoholics because they associated with people who drink. I have even seen people become drug addicts because they associated with people who do drugs. You absolutely must choose your associations very carefully. Your life depends on it! You will become who you associate with.

# Chapter Five:

## *Sowing & Reaping*

The Law Of Sowing & Reaping states that whatever you sow you will reap. If you plant (sow) an apple seed into the ground what will you reap? An apple tree. It is impossible for you to reap anything else but an apple tree if you sow an apple seed. When you sow corn, you reap corn. You reap what you sow. This is an irrefutable law that works every single time.

*Whoever sows sparingly will also reap sparingly, and whoever sows generously will also reap generously.* **2 Corinthians 9:6**

If you're trying to get rich then this verse above should make you jump for joy. Why? Because it's the law of sowing and reaping explained. The law states that if you sow a little, then you'll only reap a little, but if you sow a lot, then you'll reap a lot. So, if you want to reap a lot of money what do you need to do? You need to sow a lot of money. Pretty simple right? Well, if it's so simple then why do so few people do it? People don't understand it. That's why they don't do it. This law can change your life forever once you understand it.

I'll give you an example of how someone can become rich by operating The Law Of Sowing & Reaping. Let's say there's a man who is currently $500,000 in debt. Of that $500,000 in debt, $300,000 of it is the mortgage on his house. Another $70,000 is financed in car loans. Another $80,000 is financed in school loans, and the remaining $50,000 is credit card debt. This man has a typical nine to five job that only pays him $50,000 per year. In the natural, it's mathematically impossible for him to ever get out of debt. He doesn't make enough money, the interest is too high, and he'll run out of time (life) before he can ever pay it off. That's bad news isn't it? Well, for sinners yes, but not for Christians. You see, as a Christian, God gave us another Kingdom to operate from. He gave us laws that work every single time if we'll simply use them. The Law Of Sowing & Reaping is the only way this man will ever be able to get out of debt. So, how does he do it?

Well, the first thing he needs to do is believe that this law exists. If he doesn't believe it, then he most certainly won't ever do it. However, let's assume he believes the law will do what it says. Now, he needs to start putting The Law Of Sowing & Reaping into practice. Let's take a look at this scripture first:

*He who supplies seed to the sower and bread for food will also supply and increase your store of seed and will enlarge the harvest of your righteousness.* **2 Corinthians 9:10**

This verse explains part of The Law Of Sowing & Reaping. He needs to first know who supplies the seed (money). God is the supplier. Then, he needs to know who sows the seed. He is the sower. Now, he needs to learn how to get God to supply him with more seed. That answer is explained in this next scripture:

*Whoever can be trusted with very little can also be trusted with much, and whoever is dishonest with very little will also be dishonest with much.* **Luke 16:10**

God will bless him with more seed when he can trust him. God will trust him when he becomes a sower. He needs to sow money into The Kingdom Of God. He does this by:

1. Paying his tithes.

2. Giving offerings in faith.

3. Blessing those who are poor.

When he starts giving what little money he does have into The Kingdom Of God, he will then be able to be trusted with more. God will then start to increase him. God could increase him in a number of different ways. God could supernaturally eliminate his $500,000 debt for him free and clear. God could have his boss give him a raise. God could give him an idea to start his own business and as a business owner he could become a millionaire. Don't try to figure out how God is going to bless you because his ways are beyond finding out.

*As the heavens are higher than the earth, so are my ways higher than your ways and my thoughts than your thoughts.* **Isaiah 55:9**

Your only job is to sow seed. God gives seed to the sower. If you haven't been sowing, then that's why you haven't been reaping. However, when you do start sowing you should expect to reap a harvest.

*You will be enriched in every way so that you can be generous on every occasion, and through us your generosity will result in thanksgiving to God.* **2 Corinthians 9:11**

God wants to bless you, but he can't if you're not going to live for him. You give God legal permission to bless you financially when you sow your finances into The Kingdom Of God. As you learned earlier in this book very few people are givers and tithers.

Is it any surprise why so few people are rich? God can't trust them with a lot of money because they don't give any money from what they have now. So, God only gives to the few who are sowing seed into is Kingdom. Now, another very important part of reaping a harvest is sowing into fertile soil. Most people don't sow into fertile soil. Let's take a look at The Parable Of The Sower:

*A farmer went out to sow his seed. As he was scattering the seed, some fell along the path, and the birds came and ate it up. Some fell on rocky places, where it did not have much soil. It sprang up quickly, because the soil was shallow. But, when the sun came up the plants were scorched, and they withered because they had no root. Other seed fell among thorns, which grew up and choked the plants. Still other seed fell on good soil, where it produced a crop- a hundred, sixty or thirty times what was sown. Whoever has ears let them hear.* **Matthew 13: 3-9**

Now, what exactly does this parable mean? The seed is the word of God. The path represents someone who lives a life of sin. He hears the word, but doesn't understand it, so Satan comes and steals it from him so he doesn't believe it and get saved.

The rocky places represent someone who enjoys the word of God, but doesn't allow it into his heart. So, when temptations come his way he quickly disappears.

The thorny ground represents someone who seems to receive the word of God, but his heart is full of the lusts and pleasures of the world. Associating with the wrong people and enjoying the ways of the world takes his time and attention away from the word of God because he doesn't make it a priority.

The good soil represents someone who makes the word of God a priority in his life. He hears, understands, and receives the word of God. He allows the word of God to get down into his heart. He lives and breathes by the word of God. This man will absolutely reap a harvest; thirty, sixty, or hundred times what was sown.

*Jesus answered, it is written: Man shall not live on bread alone, but on every word that comes from the mouth of God*. **Matthew 4:4**

This person that represents good soil is the only one of the four who is truly saved because the proof of salvation is fruit. Let us finish this chapter by going to Galatians.

*Do not be deceived: God cannot be mocked. A man reaps what he sows. Whoever sows to please their flesh, from the flesh will reap destruction. Whoever sows to please the Spirit, from the Spirit will reap eternal life. Let us not become weary in doing good, for at the proper time we will reap a harvest if we do not give up. Therefore, as we have opportunity, let us do good to all people, especially those who belong to the family of believers.* **Galatians 6:7-10**

Whatever you want to reap is what you must sow. Like every law, The Law Of Sowing & Reaping works every single time. If you want to reap a lot of money, you must sow money into fertile soil. Remember that!

## Chapter Six:

## *You Must Have Faith*

The Law Of Faith states that what is impossible in the natural can be overcome by having faith in the word of God. Let's take a look at what the Holy Bible says about faith.

*Faith is confidence in what we hope for and assurance about what we do not see.* **Hebrews 11:1**

*And without faith it is impossible to please God, because anyone who comes to him must believe that he exists and that he rewards those who earnestly seek him.* **Hebrews 11:6**

Most people don't have faith and they wonder why the laws don't work in their favor. You must increase your faith if you want to experience increase in your life. To increase your faith, study the word of God.

*Consequently, **faith** comes from hearing the message, and the message is heard through the word about Christ.* **Romans 10:17**

In my personal opinion, I will say that The Law Of Faith is the most important law in existence because without faith none of the other laws will work. You must first have faith in a law in order to have that law work for your benefit. If you don't have faith that you can change your life through the words you speak, then The Law of Confession will only work against you because you'll never pay attention to your words. If you don't have faith that you can change your life with the thoughts you think, then The Law of Attraction will only work against you because you'll never pay attention to your thoughts. Each and every law must have faith attached to it, otherwise they'll work against you.

57

**Faith is what makes every law work**. You must have faith in the word of God if you want it to change your life.

*For God so loved the world that he gave his one and only Son, that whoever believes in him (**faith**) shall not perish, but have eternal life.*
**John 3:16**

If you don't have faith that God's word can heal you after you've been told by your Doctor that you're going to die from cancer, then you will absolutely die from cancer. You must believe in The Law Of Faith if you want it to heal you or change any other area of your life. Faith is what makes the impossible possible.

*Go, said Jesus, your **faith** has healed you. Immediately he received his sight and followed Jesus along the road.*
**Mark 10:52**

Remember earlier when I told you the story about Bill, the complete stranger who bought me a car? Well, my faith is what brought me that car. In the natural there was no reason in the world to believe that I was going to be able to get a car, but The Law Of Faith brought it to me in the most unimaginable way possible. When you activate The Law Of Faith it gives God the legal permission he needs in order to make miracles happen for you. Without faith, God cannot bless you. You must give him permission and you do that with your **FAITH**!

*I have chosen the way of faithfulness; I have set my heart on your laws.*
**Psalm 119:30**

Many years ago, I wanted to move from California to Florida, but I didn't have the money to do so. After some time, I finally got my faith in God high enough to pack up my tiny car and drive across the country. I only had $125, which was about $250 short of making it from California to Florida by car. However, my faith was high and I can be quite crazy at times, so I decided to take off anyway. I was honestly trusting in God to somehow provide a way for me to get all the way across the country.

I arrived in Houston, Texas on a Saturday night with only sixty-nine dollars to my name. I was exhausted from driving so many hours non-stop, so I rented the cheapest motel room I could find because I needed some rest. The motel room cost me exactly forty dollars, which meant I now only had twenty-nine dollars left. I've always been a big fan of Joel Osteen, so being in Houston, I thought I should attend the Sunday morning church service at Lakewood Church.

When it came time for the offering, I looked into my wallet and realized that I only had twenty-nine dollars left. I had a twenty-dollar bill and nine one dollar bills. I debated back and forth what I should put into the offering. Since I was filled with faith that God was going to provide a miracle for me, I decided to put in the twenty-dollar bill. I sowed that twenty dollars in complete faith and confessed as it left my hand. I was activating both The Law Of Sowing & Reaping along with The Law Of Faith! Bam! That's when miracles happen!

I sat just a few seats away from Joel and Victoria during the service. Lakewood Church was a wonderful experience. After the service was over, I walked out to my car and sat there for a few minutes with my eyes closed. I prayed that God would do something amazing.

I only had nine dollars left and I was hungry for something to eat. I started driving around and about two miles from the church there was a Chipotle. I knew I could get a bowl for just nine dollars, so that's exactly what I was going to do. While standing in line at Chipotle, I started a conversation with an older man behind me. To make a long story short, the conversation turned to me. The man asked me who I was, what I do, and why I was in Houston? I told him my current situation and when he found out that I was about to spend my last nine dollars and then I would be living in my car, he glanced at me with a puzzled look on his face. He started scratching the side of his head as if he was in shock. He then opened his mouth and started speaking in a voice of complete bewilderment. Here's what he said to me:

I have no idea why I'm doing this. I don't even know you, but I feel like I should help you. He told me that he was one of the top Brain Surgeon's in the country (he was being humble), and he just left the hospital so he could hurry and come to Chipotle for a quick bite to eat. He invited me back to the hospital so he could show me where he worked. While there, he had to leave me for a few minutes to take a phone call. When he did, I started talking to a few of the nurses who were in sight. I asked them who he was? They told me he was the nicest person they ever knew and that he was extremely wealthy. When he returned, he asked me to follow him to his house. So, I did. We sat down and talked. He said he works more than one hundred hours per week and he's hardly ever home. He said for some crazy reason he felt like he could trust me. So, he gave me a key to his house, one hundred dollars to buy myself some groceries, and told me that I could stay for as long as I wanted to.

I stayed for one week to do some sightseeing in Houston and then continued back on my journey to Florida. He gave me several hundred dollars to drive across the rest of the country. Yes, that is a true story! That's what The Law Of Faith can do!

I decided to share some of my real life experiences with you in this book to show you that these laws really do work. Throughout my life, these laws have worked for my benefit most of the time. The times that they've worked for me, rather than against me were the times when I had faith. My faith is what gave God legal permission to intercede on my behalf. Do you think it was luck or a mere coincidence that I landed in the Chipotle line exactly where I did? No, not at all! That was God directing my steps. That was God guiding me to be at the right place at the right time. Do you think it was luck or a mere coincidence that the wealthy Brain Surgeon took a break from the hospital at the exact time that he did? No, not at all! That was a divinely orchestrated event by the creator of the universe.

The Law Of Faith is what activates **EVERY** other law in existence! The Holy Bible tells us to live by faith, not by sight. If I would have lived by what I could see with my natural eyes Satan would have deceived me and made me sad, depressed, and hopeless. However, I lived by faith. Look at what this scripture says:

*As the body without the spirit is dead, so faith without deeds is dead.*
**James 2:26**

I could have said I was in faith, but then just stayed in California until I saved five hundred dollars to drive across the country. If I would have done that I might still be in California today. I took massive, immediate action! By taking massive, immediate action, which is something very few people do, I proved that I was in faith. Someone who isn't in faith will never take action. My faith is what allowed these amazing stories to take place in my life. Not only do you need to have faith, but you also need to take massive action! Remember this: **FAITH WITHOUT ACTION IS DEAD**!

# Chapter Seven:

## *It's Time To Get Rich*

Now that you know The 6 Financial Laws Of Success, it's time to start using them to get rich. I want you to know that it's God's desire for you to be rich. It's a sin to be poor. The best thing you can do to help the poor is **NOT** be one of them. God wants you to be rich so you can be a blessing to others. Now that you know the laws, you must activate them with faith.

Life is better when you have an abundance of money. Imagine how it would feel to pay cash for your cars. Imagine how it would feel to pay cash for your houses. Imagine how it would feel to be completely debt free. Imagine how it would feel when you never have to worry about money again. Money rules this world.

*A feast is made for laughter, wine makes life merry, and **money** is the answer for everything.*
**Ecclesiastes 10:19**

If you went around like I often do and started telling people that **money is the answer for everything**, they would condemn you and tell you you're going to hell. However, that's exactly what the Holy Bible says. The reason why 98% of the world's population is poor is because they don't understand the financial laws I just shared with you in this book. There is absolutely nothing beneficial about being poor. Being poor is a disgrace to you, your family, and to society. It's actually very selfish to be poor. By being poor you're only thinking about yourself. If you only need $50,000 to live on, then start making a million dollars and give the rest away to people who need it.

Having a lot of money is a good thing. Money allows us to be a blessing to others. An abundance of money reduces stress. An abundance of money would prevent most of the fighting that occurs between spouses. An abundance of money would prevent most of the divorces in this world. An abundance of money would prevent most of the crimes that people commit. Say this out loud: **I love money! The more money I have the more people I can bless!**

Now, I'm going to get personal with you for a minute. You just learned The 6 Financial Laws Of Success, but you can't just read a book and think you're going to become a millionaire. You have to make some changes in your life. What do I mean? Well, let me ask you a question: **In your life right now, are you an employee or a business owner?**

You may not want to hear this, but I'm going to tell you anyway. If I don't tell you I wouldn't be doing anything to help you. If you're an employee, you will **NEVER** get rich! You must become a business owner if you want to get rich. You must! This is 100% non-negotiable! It's impossible to get rich as an employee. Talk is cheap, but documentation beats conversation every day of the week. Numbers never lie. So, let me prove it to you with cold hard facts. There's only two classes of people in the world. **Rich** and **Poor**. Even the Holy Bible talks about this:

*Rich and poor have this in common; The Lord is the Maker of them all.*
**Proverbs 22:2**

*For God does not show favoritism.*
**Romans 2:11**

If The Lord is the maker of both the rich and the poor and he loves us all the same, then why is only 2% of the world's population rich? The answer is **choice**. People either choose to be rich or they choose to be poor. There isn't any other choice to make. It's one or the other and they make this choice based on what they do. Every employee knows that business owners make more money. Every employee in the world knows they can't get rich at their job. Let me prove it by looking at the facts!

**Fact**: 98% of the world's population are employees.

**Fact:** 98% of the world's population earn linear income.

**Fact:** 98% of the world's population live paycheck to paycheck.

**Fact**: 2% of the world's population are business owners.

**Fact**: 2% of the world's population earn residual income.

**Fact**: 2% of the world's population are wealthy.

Believe it or not, the only difference between the rich and the poor is the way they think. One of the financial laws you just learned talks about this: **The Law Of Attraction**. You see, poor people are always thinking about what they **DON'T** want. They think about the annoying alarm clock waking them up when it's still dark outside, which they hate. They think about going to work at their dead end job, which they hate. They think about the tiny paycheck they're going to get, which they hate. They think about all the bills they're going to get in the mail, which they hate.

However, rich people are always thinking about what they **WANT**. They think about waking up when they're done sleeping, which they love. They think about working on their business whenever they feel like it, which they love. They think about the millions of dollars they earn, which they love. They think about all the things they can buy because they don't have any bills, which they love. Both the rich and the poor get exactly what they constantly think about. That's The Law Of Attraction. Let me show you the differences between the way the rich and the poor think:

**Employees think**: I just got a two dollar an hour raise at my job.

**Business Owners think**: I just took my company public and made over two hundred million dollars.

**Employees think**: I get thirty minutes a day for lunch.

**Business Owners think**: I'll take as much time as I want for lunch.

**Employees think**: My job gives me a steady paycheck and benefits.

**Business Owners think**: Benefits? I'm a Multi-Millionaire. What the heck do I need benefits for?

**Employees think**: I get two paid weeks of vacation per year.

**Business Owners think**: I take vacations all year round and my income increases while I'm gone.

**Employees think**: Honey, let's go to Applebee's for dinner. I'll pay with the credit card.

**Business Owners think**: Honey, let's hop in the jet and fly to France for dinner. I'll pay with cash.

These are real thoughts that the rich and the poor have. Obviously, you can see the difference. The only way you're going to get rich is by thinking differently and becoming a business owner. If you've been an employee working for someone else your entire life, you're going to have to move to the other side of the cashflow quadrant and start a business. You'll continue to remain poor if you don't. So, the question you must answer is: **What type of business do you start?**

Since this is my book and I want to help you get rich, let me give you my personal advice. I truly practice what I preach. So, I'm only going to tell you to do something that I've already done and continue to do. I've owned many different types of businesses throughout my life, so here's some important things you want to look for in a potential business model.

Start a **home-based business** of some kind. This will allow you to work from home, work whenever you want, call your own shots, and spend a lot of time with your family.

Start a business that pays you **residual income**. Residual income is money that comes in long after the work has been finished. Without residual income, you'll have to work for the rest of your life.

Start a business that **you can scale** all over the world and that can impact millions of people's lives.

Find a **successful mentor** who has the experience to coach you.

It took me thirty-five years to find a business model that offered all four of these benefits. That business is: **ACN: NETWORK MARKETING**.

By becoming a home-based business owner with ACN, you have all the following benefits available to you:

-Get to work from home.

-Get to earn residual income.

-Get to build a global business.

-Get to have a successful mentor.

Let me tell you why I think starting your own home-based business with ACN is the greatest business model you could ever start:

1. Very low start-up cost. At much less than $1,000 to start, you can make your money back and become profitable in less than a week.

2. No employees to deal with. ACN hires, trains, pays, and handles all the employees that work for you on the back end so you can just focus on building your business.

3. Unlimited residual income potential. Unlike working at a job, with ACN there is no limit to how much money you can earn.

4. You can build a global company from the comfort of your own home. ACN is currently on four different continents and continuing to expand every single year.

5. You can join my team and work with me. I will personally teach you everything you need to know for you to become successful.

6. You get to help people change their lives for a living. There's no better feeling than being able to help people:
-fire their boss.
-get out of debt.
-become financially free.
-travel all over the world.
-spend more time with their family.

I have never seen a business model that offers so many positive benefits, yet has such a low start-up cost. ACN has truly changed my life in every area imaginable and I know it can do the same for you. Let me ask you some brief questions:

-Do you ever watch tv?

-Do you have a cell phone?

-Do you ever use the internet?

-Do you use gas and/or electricity?

-Do you have any valuables that are worth securing?

If you answered "yes" to any of these questions, then you're already a part of ACN. Don't you think you should make it official and start getting paid for doing the same things that I do? If you're confused, allow me to explain.

ACN is the world's largest provider of essential services that **YOU** and **EVERYONE YOU KNOW** already use every single day. Instead of paying these bills every month for the rest of your life, ACN allows you to get paid when people all over the world pay these bills every month for the rest of their lives. Which one sounds better to you: pay bills every single month, or get paid when people pay bills every single month? Exactly! It's a complete no brainer. If you're interested in learning more about how you can start getting paid residual income every single month for the rest of your life when people all over the world pay their monthly bills, simply watch the video on my website and then give me a call: www.ChangeYourLifeOvernight.com

If you enjoyed reading this book, here's more books by the author:

-Sell Your First Book

-Vision Board Success

-My Inspiring True Life Story

-Money Meditation Manifestation

-Entrepreneurship: Money, Wealth, & Prosperity

-Network Marketing Success, Failure, & Everything In Between

-How To Lose Weight With Intermittent Fasting

Success: The Secret To Becoming Happy, Healthy, And Wealthy

-How To Make Money As An Author Selling Your Books On Amazon

All books can be purchased from:

www.amazon.com/author/fitchristophermitchell

www.ingramcontent.com/pod-product-compliance
Lightning Source LLC
Chambersburg PA
CBHW072040190526
45165CB00018B/1283